A PILGRIM'S FAITH

A PILGRIM'S FAITH

"These all died in faith (according to faith), not having received the promises, but having seen them afar off, and were persuade of them, and embraced them, and confessed that they were strangers and pilgrims on earth."
Hebrews 11:13

BOOK 2
OF THE FAITH SERIES

Dr. R Michael Baldock

Ordering Information:

For orders and inquiries, please contact:
1-888-404-1388
www.goldtouchpress.com
book.orders@goldtouchpress.com

Printed in the United States of America

CONTENTS

SPECIAL THANKS

I want to extend a special thanks to those who have encouraged me to keep writing and to those who have been supportive of this ministry. To Apostle Anthony and first Lady Connie Williams, Pastors of the Lion of the Tribe of Judah Ministries. It was that great ministry that got me started publishing my writings. To Pastors, Tim and Deanna Agee and the great congregation of the Sanctuary Church in, Beech Grove/Indianapolis, Indiana. To Mel and Erin Glenn who has been so supportive especially Erin who put up with all the hours Mel and I have spent to gather. To Mark and Marcella Agee, without, which this project could not have happened. Then, of course, my beautiful wife Julie, who has been by my side for the last thirty-six years. Thanks to all of the people that God has placed in our path to keep this ministry alive and progressing!

Thank You So Very Much
May God's Richest Blessings Be Yours
Dr. Mike

INTRODUCTION

In the great 'Hall of Fame of Faith' (Heb. 11) the writer speaks plainly of those who were pilgrims in the faith. They were a people who lived their life by faith in the promises of God. They lived looking for a better country! They looked toward the 'Cross!'

"Theses all died in faith (looking toward the cross) not having received the promises, but having seen them afar off, and were persuaded of them, and embraced them, and confessed that they were strangers and pilgrims on the earth

"For they say such things declare plainly that they seek a country."

"And truly, if they had been mindful of that country from whence they came out, they might have had opportunity to have returned."

"But they now desire a better country, that is, a heavenly: wherefore God is not ashamed to be called their God: for He hath prepared for them a city." Hebrews 11:13-16

The above passage of scripture reveals the mindset of the 'Pilgrim's of the faith. Within the following pages we are going to examine the attributes of **'A Pilgrim of Faith!'**

Rand House Webster's College Dictionary, defines a pilgrim as; a person who journeys, a long distance to some sacred place as an act of religious devotion, a traveler or wanderer, in a foreign place.

These Pilgrim's of faith were traveling for more than a religious fulfillment, they were searching for spiritual fulfillment! When I think of a pilgrim, I think of a person who blazes a trail; an adventurous person; one who is fearless; an explorer. A pilgrim is a person who is not afraid to take chances, make changes, and/or do something different than thee ordinary. A pilgrim's faith will take a person to places they have never been. When fear does arrive, the pilgrim will keep their goal in front of them and not get detoured.

The day that a person receives Jesus Christ as their Lord and Savior, they will begin their journey of faith, that is, **'A Pilgrim's Faith!'** As believers, we are pilgrims traveling through this life, and what a travel it is! Remember, the believer is not of this world, even though we are in it (John 15:19). It is the way we travel in faith that will determine our destiny and where we travel that determines our spiritual success!

When I think of a pilgrim, I am reminded of a song recorded by Steven Curtis Chapman, **'The Great Adventure!'** There is a phrase within this great song that reminds me the **'The Christian Pilgrimage!' It says, 'Saddle up your horses we've got a trail to blaze!'** What a Challenge!

Within the following pages, I want to extend a challenge, you, the believer to begin blazing the trail of **'A Pilgrims Faith!'** I will be sharing with you some of the things concerning and walking in a **"Pilgrims'** kind of faith. Within each proceeding chapter we will take you on a journey that will reveal a new dimension of faith! So, let's get started!

CHAPTER 1

The Pilgrimage!

There was a group of English separatist who became known as the Pilgrims. The leader of the Pilgrims was a man by the name of William Bradford. They disagreed with the religious teachings of the Church of England.

The Church of England was in concert with the Government of England. King James 1 was the head of both the country and the church. Anyone who did not belong to the Church of England was guilty of treason

They originally left England aboard the Mayflower in July of 1620 for America to escape religious persecution. While traveling with a ship called Speedwell they had to turn back twice because of the Speedwell developing leaks. After deciding to leave her companion ship behind they boarded the Mayflower and left once again on September 6, 1620. They knew when they set sail for the New World, that they would face many difficulties. Even facing what seemed to be impossible odds, they moved forward believing it was possible to reach their destiny.

While crossing the ocean was long and difficult and many thought they would not ever see land. While facing what seemingly to be insurmountable odds, they moved forward believing it was possible to reach their destiny

They left England in search of a safe place to practice their faith and en joy religious freedom. As stated earlier The state Church of England brought persecution when all the while England became a political boiling pot.

On November 9, 1620 they saw land to the New World. They dropped anchor at Cap Cod, which is now Massachusetts. They now began to live their dream.

If it was not for Pilgrims looking for a better country with better living we would all still be living caves somewhere. It is the hopes, dreams and the tenacity (Faith) to pursue something better. The same is true for the Christian of today. We cannot allow ourselves to be swallowed up in mediocrity. Complacency has no place for the Child of God! The Apostle Paul said;

> ***"Not as though I had already attained (reached full growth and maturity), either were already perfect (not living in sinless perfection and not complete in reaching my goal): but I follow after (in eager pursuit), if that I may apprehend (seize) that for which I am apprehended of Christ Jesus. (receiving what Jesus Christ did at the cross and all its benefits)"***

"Brethren, I count not myself to have apprehended (seized it all): but this one thing I do, forgetting those things which are behind, and reaching forth unto those things which are before."

"I press toward the mark (the goal before me) for the prize of the high calling of God in Christ Jesus." Philippians 3:12-14

In the above passage, Paul revels some important information that is of great help, while the believer is is going after what is ahead of them.

1. **Forgetting those things that are behind!** We cannot allow our past to hinder our future. Paul was also referring to not allowing his flesh to dictate to him along with not working within his own strength, knowledge and ability. He learned as we must learn also that the only way to pursue the will of God is by the leading of the Holy Spirit! The believer will never find favor with God trying to do it their own way!

2. **Reaching forth unto those things which are before!** It is a must that the believer wear what I call, **'Spiritual Blinders.'** When a horse is in a race, they have blinders on that keep their surroundings from impairing them to remain focused on what is ahead, **'The Finish line!'** As believers we must give our full attention on what is ahead of us, which is, **'the victories that Jesus Christ gained at the Cross!' (Luke 9:23)**

3. **Pressing toward the mark!** The word **'press,'** is from the Greek word **'Dioko,'** meaning to follow after. Literally, **'pursuing'** (as one would (their) a calling). The word **'mark,'** is from the Greek word **'Skopos,'** meaning to look toward a goal, give heed. Used as a mark at the goal or the end of a race. The goal should include reaching for moral and spiritual excellence!

4. **For the prize of the high calling of God in Christ Jesus.** The prize is that which is within the, **'Finished Work of Jesus Christ at Calvary!'** The word **'high,'** is from the Greek word **'Ano,'** meaning above, in a higher place, of a location in a higher place. Paul was referring to a place within Jesus Christ that is high above all principalities, powers and might. (Eph. 1:18-23; 2:4-6)

The word **'calling,'** is from the Greek word **'Kiesis,'** which is derived from the word **'Kaleo'** meaning, to call, a calling, a condition of employment. It also suggests being called by name either for a vocation or destination, which can only be d the found within Jesus Christ and the victories He has won! The victories and calling of Jesus Christ come from the **'Cross which is the means,'** and **'Jesus Christ which is the (our) source!'**

When you begin (or already in) your Pilgrimage you will be faced with the winds and waves of the sea, here will be rough travel however, there will be smooth places as well. In your quest for all that Jesus Christ paid for at Calvary, keep your mind right (Romans 12:2) keep your sight on the goal and follow the leading of the Holy Spirit (Romans chapters 6 and 8)! You too, will reach the **'high calling of God in Christ Jesus!"**

CHAPTER 2

Pilgrims Are 'Dream Carriers'

Most of the amenities (if all) that we enjoy today are the results of someone dreaming a dream. That is, dreaming with a great desire for something better. Those dreams became a trail that was blazes and the dream became a reality.

God has placed within each of us the ability to dream; the ability to think and ponder, on the desire to do and accomplish in life. For dreams, to come alive, it takes hard work and dedication.

To dream is to see yourself occupying a place, or doing something that you are not currently involved in. It is a mental picture of you accomplishing a goal. The greater accomplishment is not the ability to dream, but it is the tenacity to hold onto that dream and make it a reality. It doesn't matter who agrees, disagrees, or who doesn't understand the content of your dream. What really matters, is you seeing that dream through until it reaches its full potential! You and God are in control of the outcome!

Allow me to reminisce for a moment. I remember back in the very early 1950's, when we got our first Television. I realize that I am dating myself!) We only had three channels on television, it was still enjoyable even when not all of the channels were working, remember when my grandmother got her first wringer washer. Now that was a big deal! It meant that we longer had to wash clothes by hand! Then, we really moved up! Grandma got twin tubs to go with the washer! I realize, some of you have no idea what a wringer washer and twin tubs are. But, having them sure made washing clothes easier. It was progress in action!

When it came wash day (that was usually on Monday), after washing the laundry we still had to hang the clothes up to dry. Once they were dry by that good ole fresh country air, we would gather them up. Upon bringing the clothes into the house grandma would do something at the time I did realize why. She would sprinkle the clothes with water and roll them up and put them in the refrigerator. Even now, that sounds so silly, but that's the way it was done. You might be asking, **"Why wet them down and roll them up and place them in the refrigerator after they were dry?"** Great question! In those days, everything was ironed. So, in order to keep the clothes fresh, while waiting to iron them. Wow! We really did have it made then! Oh, and just a side note, we had no idea what an air condition was!

We have made a lot of improvements since then! We now have automatic washers and driers, microwave ovens, remote controls for television, with, hundreds of channels. We now have cell phones (back in the day we had phones but for the most part they were party lines), air conditioning in home and the car. We also have automobiles that practically drive themselves. We have advanced a lot way in my lifetime.

There are so many amenities now that has made living more convenient and enjoyable. When you think of the things that we now have, think on this, they all began as a dream in someone's mind. Someone put their blood, sweat, and tears, along with a lot of hard work and determination in order to make their dream (invention) a reality.

What is the difference in those that dream a dream and those that live a dream? I am convinced that the answer is found within the faith, determination, and courage of the individual. It is their faith and courage to dare take the steps needed to make their dreams (goals) a reality!

These are also separated by trying something without being held back by the fear of failure. It is such fear that has stymied many from accomplishing their dream. I heard said many years ago, **"The cemetery is filled with unfulfilled dreams!"** Within every cemetery there are songs never written nor sang. There are books never written and sermons never preached! Yes, the cemetery is filled with of unfulfilled dreams!

When you begin your journey to fulfill your dreams, you can be assured that you will meet resistance. There is no doubt that setbacks will come your way. People, places and things will try to keep you from accomplishing the dreams and goals that are ahead of you! When the come, keep this in mind, when you suffer a setback you have one of two choices; **1. You can sit-back or 2. You can make a comeback!** It is those who keep coming back, after being knocked down time and again, that make their dreams a reality!

<u>Dreamers</u>

The list of dreamers is endless, some of which we know and others that have long been forgotten. There is one dreamer that comes to mind, his name is George Washington Carver. His dreams and tenacity revolutionized farming in the south. The story is; George asked God to show him the secret of the Universe. God's reply was (or so it has been said), **"I'll not show you the secret of the universe. However, I will show you the secret of the peanut!"** God proceeded to tell him, **"Take a peanut in your hand!"** Mr. Carver, following God's instructions, held a peanut in his hand. With the peanut in hand God gave further instructions. God instructed him to take the peanut apart, which he did. Now, while holding the peanut he had taken apart, God told him to put it back together again! God was now going to show George the **"secret of the peanut!"** When putting the torn apart peanut back together there came well over three hundred ways (products) that the peanut useful. In one of his periodicals, he shared with the farming community, **"How to grow the peanut and 105 ways of preparing it for mans consumption!"**

George was also credited with revealing, when, what and how to can and preserve fruits and vegetables in the home! Not only was he a great dreamer, but, he was also known as a scientist. It was his **'Christian Faith' (a Pilgrim's Faith)** that gave him the strength and courage to do what he did. There are far too many things he accomplished that changed things for the better to list here. However, he never ceased to dream a dream and to live the dream!

There was another man (dreamer) that few even remember or know about his name was A. Philip Randolph. Mr. Randolph had a dream (a vision) for a massive, orderly, dignified parade that favored civil rights through the streets of our Nation's capital. Randolph's proposed march set for 1941 never came into fruition (Source Black Americans Achievements). However, his dream did fully take place.

In 1957, there was a man who would carry out Mr. Randolph's dream. His name was Martin Luther King Jr. He envisioned (dreamed) of the masses marching in Washington D.C. Dr. King's dream was much larger than, Randolph's.

It was on August 28, 1963, when a much larger demonstration than one could imagine, took place. There were about 250,000 people from diverse backgrounds, came together to march for **'Civil Rights!'** They marched from the Washington Monument to the Lincoln Monument. It was there, that Randolph, now at the age of 74, would introduce several speakers. It was after Mahalia Jackson sang the old spiritual, **'I've been buked and I've been scorned, 'Scorned,"** that Randolph was honored to introduce the **'Moral Leader of the Nation, Dr. Martin Luther King Jr.'** who was the last speaker of the day. It was there, that Dr. King delivered a speech which still echoes across this Great Nation! Within the content of King's speech, was his dream. He dreamed of a time when **"little black boys and black girls would be able to join hands with little white boys and white girls as sisters and brothers!"** He also dreamed of, **"freedom ringing from every mountain top!"** It was twenty-six years after Randolph's dream, he not only saw his dream come true, but, he was involved in that dream!

Several years ago, I was invited to speak at a Martin Luther King Jr. memorial. The speaker before me made the following statement, **"It would be great if Dr. King was alive, to see his dream becoming a reality!"** Howbeit, his dream is coming along slowly, but we are making progress. I followed the speaker before me and I said, **"I don't me to contradict the speaker before me, However, Dr. King did see his dream!"** That dream was rooted within his heart! He proclaimed it from a **'Pilgrim's Faith Perspective!' Faith has a way to see long before the natural mind and eyes!**

Your Dreams Will Draw An Attack

You can be assured that once you begin to dream and put feet to that dream, it will draw an attack from the enemy. Often times that attack occurs because the enemy knows something that you don't!

Within the scriptures, there are many people in which God gave dreams. Time and space will not allow us to reveal every dream and dreamer. However, there is the story of one particular person whose was referred to as, **'The Dreamer."** His name was Joseph (Gen. 37). Before Joseph ever shared the dream that God gave to him, his brothers hated him because of their father's love for for Joseph. Because of their lack of understanding their hatred deepened toward him when he shared the dream. As Joseph proclaimed what God gave him, their hatred ran even deeper. Matter of fact, the dream infuriated them.

Because of their anger and hatred toward Joseph, they began to attack him. Their attack on him came with a fury! They wanted to kill him! Upon hearing of their plot to kill him, his brother Reuben, put a stop to him being killed. Instead of killing Joseph, they tossed him into a pit and left him there for dead. The Midianite merchantmen were passing was by and found him and drew him from the pit. They sold him to the Ishmeelites for twenty pieces of silver and they brought him to Egypt. He was then sold to Potiphar. While serving Potiphar, he was falsely accused of making sexual advances to Potiphar's wife. He was then thrown into prison. What an attack!

It was only after his endurance of these many hardships, that he was placed in the Palace as the Viceroy for Pharaoh1 It was within this position that he ultimately ended up fulfilling the dream that God gave him many years before! Please understand, I am in no way suggesting this kind of attack upon everyone who pursues their dreams. However, as I said earlier, you can expect some kind of attack.

I have noticed, in my own life and ministry, that when I begin to act upon faith and pursue what God has placed before me, there is some kind of attack. Just as Joseph faced opposition because of his God-given dreams, so will you! I am not trying to be negative, however, I do want you to be aware and prepared. Any time the believer begins to move in faith and the favor of God, an attack will come! It is sad to say, but, there are people who cannot stand to see others succeed in life!

It should never be that way, but their jealousy becomes a contending attack! You would think everyone in the Church would rejoice when you are walking in a **'Pilgrim's Faith,'** but that is just not true! The truth is, there will always be those that will despise you. This is especially true when you begin walking in the blessings of the Lord. I have received some of my most viscous attacks from other believers. You must guard yourself from the haters!

I don't know who, or what, may be standing in the way of you accomplishing your dream! However, I do know this, if you will continue to hold onto that dream (vision) and dare not to give up, you can, and you will accomplish what is before you! You might as well get prepared through the Word, for the obstacles, they will come and sometimes it will be one after another! But, be of good cheer, face each obstacle with courage, without wavering in your faith, and you too, will make it to the **'Palace' (the place where God wants you to be!)** Whatever you do, do not allow the opposition of haters stop you from pursuing your dream!

Within the scriptures, we find the patriarchs of faith, who paved the way for those coming after them. Such believers as, Abraham, Isaac, Jacob, and many others that had great faith in God and His promises! Those promises were within the Cross and the finished work of Jesus Christ, which was yet to come! It was their faith that allowed them to dream a dream! It was their **'Pilgrim kind of faith'** that kept them searching for a better country and for a city whose builder and maker was God!

While these great men and women of faith looked toward the **'Cross,'** as their object of faith, the believer of today looks back at the **'Cross and the Finished Work of Jesus Christ!'** Every believer now has before them, the opportunity to walk in the **'Benefits of the Cross!'** See Luke 9:23

Just as the great men and women who went before us, we too, can dream a dream and go forth with faith and courage!

Dreamers Are Risk Takers!

When the pilgrims set sail for a new land (America) the faced difficulties on their journey. They endured hardships, which often times they were intense. The hardships were not over when they landed. It was their dream for a better place, with a religious freedom, that enabled them to endure the hardships. They were willing to face whatever would come their way. The necessary risks they would take was a small price to pay to see their dreams come to pass!

When I think of risk takers I am reminded of Simon Peter. While they were toiling in the sea Jesus appeared to them. When Jesus said to Peter, **"Come,"** he immediately got out of the boat. He began walking on the water in the midst of the storm! The scriptures do not reveal how far he walked, but, he did walk on the water going toward Jesus. It was when, for a brief moment took his eyes off of Jesus, he began to sink.

I have heard so many preachers and teachers belittle Peter for his failure. I don't believe that Peter failed at all. When he began to sink, he cried out to Jesus to save him, and upon his cry for help Jesus Christ lifted him up! I am convinced the he and Jesus walked on water back to the boat!

It was at this time that Jesus took the opportunity to teach a life lesson. When they the boat began to teach. While looking at Peter, Jesus said, **"O ye of little faith!"** This term is from the Greek word, **'Oligopistos'** this is a compound word, the first part, **'Oligos'** means, little, small, brief, puny. The second word **'Pistos'** meaning, faith. Together the word **'Oligopistos'** is defined as; little faith, trusting to little, insufficient faith. With these definitions we can come to the conclusion that it is, lacking trust or confidence in Jesus Christ.

It is important to notice, Peter began his walk in faith, howbeit brief. The lesson here is, one must keep their faith focused on the correct object. What Peter did is called, **'Misplaced Faith.'** (we will go into a greater detail in the study book of, **"Misplaced!'**)

It may seem easy to is criticize Peter for taking his eyes off of Jesus for a brief moment. But, what about the other eleven disciples, who didn't budge, nor attempt to get out of the boat? I am convinced that fear gripped their heart so much it kept them from making a move. I also realize that Jesus spoke directly to Peter. But, the entire boat was filled with fear do to the storm they were in. Whatever your perception may be concerning Peter, we must agree **'He was a risk taker!' This was certainly an act of a 'Pilgrims faith!'** This is the kind of faith that responds to the Word of God, no matter what the flesh is saying!

There is a lesson in this story for the believer of today. The focus of our (your) faith must be in the correct object. That object must **'cross and the finished work of Jesus Christ!'** This may seem to be a risk but actually it is faith in the Grace of God!

Another risk taker that comes to mind is found in **1 Kings 17.** God had spoken to a widow in Zarephath to sustain the Prophet

Elijah. When Elijah arrived, she was in the process of making the last bit of food she had. Her and her son, where going to eat, what was to be their last meal, and then they were going to wait upon death.

Elijah spoke to her saying, feed me first, and God will supply and take care of you and your son! She took the **'Risk'** and stepped out in faith! The scriptures declare, that her meal barrel, and her cruse of oil never wasted! Once again, this is a prime example of someone walking in **'A Pilgrims kind of Faith!'**

When we keep our eyes and faith on the correct object, which is the **'Cross and the Finished Work of Jesus Christ,'** what seems to be a risk is actually faith and the Grace of God!

We have witnesses that this kind of faith works!

> *Wherefore seeing we are compassed about with so great a cloud of witnesses, let us lay aside every weight, and the sin which doth so easily beset us, and let us run with patience the race that is set before us,"*
>
> *"Looking unto Jesus the author and finisher of our faith; who for the joy that was set before Him endured the cross, despising the shame, and is set down at the right hand of the throne of God." Hebrews 12:1-2*

Since the scriptures declare that we are surrounded by a cloud of witnesses, that alone should move us into a territory (spiritually) where we have never been! It is time to lay aside whatever may be holding you back from moving forward!

This is the 'Pilgrim kind of faith!' It is a faith, which, puts the flesh aside and respond to the Word of God that will take you and I into places we have never been before!

The Communication of a Dreamer

1. **They look beyond the impossible and see the possible!**

2. **They see the invisible!**

3. **They obtain the unobtainable!**

4. **They say, "I can do that!"**

This is exactly what correct faith does! You cannot be a coward and continue to pursue (follow) after your dream! I am convinced that the fear of failure is the number one enemy against you accomplishing your dreams!

You have a choice today! Make the choice to dream a dream and to live that dream! I challenge you, today, to put in motion the faith to live the dream that is within you! **GO FOR IT! DREAM BIG!**

CHAPTER 3

A Pioneer (Pilgrim) of Faith

Abraham is often referred to as the **'Father of Faith'** and rightfully so. However, I want to explore another man who I consider a **'pioneer of faith.'** His name is, **'Enoch.'**

Enoch was the seventh from Adam and the son of Jared. Enoch also begat Methuselah which means *'the deluge (the flood) shall be sent when he is dead'* and of course, Methuselah lived 969 years.

When we look into the life of Enoch we will discover some facts about him that you may not have known. There are five books that are attributed to Enoch as being the author;

1.   The Book of Wathchers.

2.   The Book of Similtudes.

3.   The Astronomical Book

4. The Book of Dreams

5. The Epistle of Enoch

The complete volume survives in Epthiopic, However, there are sections that appear in Greek.

Enoch walked (before) with God. Enoch was possibly 65 years of age when he began his relationship with God. He lived 365 years. It was during those 300 years that Enoch **'walked (before) with God' (Genesis 5:24).** While walking with God I am sure that God shared His character along with many other things to this great man! Enoch's walk of faith with God certainly separated him from any others.

There is little doubt that God shared the coming **'flood'** with Enoch. Think about this, Adam was still alive at this time, he may have been somewhere between 600 and 700 years old. Adam lived another 230 years. During Adams lifetime it was very possible that Enoch witnessed and gave testimony to Adam about the upcoming event (the flood).

Enoch witnessed (prophesied) for God. His witness included sharing the revelation, of Jesus Christ returning with ten thousand saints and executing judgment, which will be at the, **'Battle of Armagddon' (Revelation 14:14-20; 19:11-21)**

> *"And Enoch also, the seventh from Adam, prophesied of these, saying, Behold, the Lord cometh with ten thousand saints,"*

> *"To execute judgment upon all that are ungodly among them of all their ungodly deeds which*

they have ungodly committed, and of all their hard speeches which ungodly sinners have spoken against Him."

These are murmurers, complainers, walking after their own liust; and their mouth speaketh great swelling words, having men's persons in admiration because of advantage." Jude 14-16

In this passage, Jude quotes from the apocryphal Book of Enoch. Although this book was not included in the canon Scripture, early church historians wrote that the church accepted it as a valid source of information. Therefore, it is plausible to conclude that Jud, writing under the inspiration of the Holy Spirit, used this prophecy of Enoch as a means of describing those false teachers who sought to lead astray believers from true faith in Christ.

For some time this passage was a chief reason for the Book of Jude's rejection from the canon of scripture. However, by the fourth century A.D., Jude's letter had been fully accepted tire church. Hebrew Greek Key Study Bible Key Notes

<u>Enoch pleased God!</u>

"By faith Enoch was translated that he should not see death; and it was not found, because God had translated him: for before his translation he had this testimony, that he pleased God." Hebrews 11:5

The above passage of scripture is the reason why I consider Enoch as the **'pioneer of faith!'** He lived during a time of man's rebellion against God. Man was full of himself and lived ungodly, immoral, wicked imagination and thoughts. However, he was separated from all of ungodliness and gave his life as a servant to (of) the Lord.

I am also convinced, during those three hundred years walking and talking with God, that God also revealed to Enoch the **'Cross and what Jesus Christ would accomplish there.'** I also am convinced that Enoch had his faith in the **'Cross and what Jesus Christ would there do!**

As Enoch looked toward the **'Cross'** the believer today is to put all their faith in the **'Cross and the Finished Work of Jesus Christ.' (Hebrews 12:1-2)**

I have heard the story of Enoch's translation put this way;

Enoch and God were on their daily walk. God was given Enoch one revelation after another. While being engrossed with what God was revealing, Enoch said, **'God it is getting late, so I need to go home.'** God responded saying, **Enoch, we are closer to my home then yours, so, just come home with me!'**

It may not have happened that way but it makes for a great conversation piece!

> *"And Enoch walked with God: and he was not:*
> *for God took him." Genesis 5:24*

<u>WHAT A GREAT MAN OF GOD!</u>

ONLY TO BE THAT CLOSE TO GOD!

CHAPTER 4

Pilgrims Go Before they Know!

What I mean by the phrase, **'Pilgrims go before they know'** the faith of a pilgrim is a faith that does not have to know all of the details of the journey ahead of them. If you are the kind of person who must analyze everything before you become involved, it will be difficult for you to operate in this kind of faith.

As I referred to in the last chapter, when the pilgrims boarded ships to come to America, they did so because of a dream of a better place. When they left shores behind them, they really did not know what trails they would face. Yet, they launched out anyway! They were drawn by their dreams.

Those who live and walk in a **'Pilgrims Faith'** will go before they know all of the details. I have come to realize this in my own life. I learned this by how the Holy Spirit would speak to me. Most of the time, He would say, **"It is time for you to remove yourself from this place i.e. point A. Then, I will take you to a new place, i.e. point B**. This was without revealing to me the venture between these two places. Most of the time I didn't have any idea where **'Point B'** was, nor did I have any idea how I was going to arrive there. I knew very little, if anything at all what was ahead of me in this journey between these two points. All I knew was, the Holy Spirit gave me a directive, and He would lead the way. The one thing I had to fight was not allowing my feelings along with my ideas and opinions getting in the way! Ma y I say, to this point (it has been fifty years) it has been a great ride. Oh, sure, there have been some rocky places but God has always brought through with victory!

Let's take a few moments and examine two great men that walked this kind of path. Let's look at Noah first. When God looked and saw the heart and minds full of vain imaginations and being full of evil. Man continued in that evil, wicked way (Gen. 6:1-7). It was then, God called a man by the name of Noah (Gen. 6:8). God revealed to Noah that He was going to destroy all flesh upon the earth. It was then that God instructed this great man to build an Ark. The promise that Noah was given was he and his family would be saved. That included his wife, three sons and their wives. God was going to establish a covenant with Noah (Gen.6-7)

Noah began to build the Ark, while listening intently to God's direction. **Noah moved with a reverent fear (Heb.11:7)!**

> *"By faith Noah being warned of God of things not seen as yet, moved with fear, prepared an ark to the saving of his house; by the which he condemned the world, and became heir of righteousness which is by faith."*

Noah built the Ark as God instructed him, and he did so with a faith that was full of reverence fear to God! Just as anyone walking in a **'Pilgrims Faith,'** Noah took it a step at a time, for he was walking new territory! He never allowed himself to get entrapped by looking too far ahead. He was at **'Point A' and only God could get him to point B, wherever that might be.**

Noah did not wait until the first raindrop to fall before he started building the Ark. He began building before it rained! Noah did as God instructed him, and saved the earth from total destruction. He operated in a **'Pilgrims Kind of Faith!'**

Without fail, every time the Word is spoken it demands action. It was by faith that Noah put in action what God had spoken, even though, he did not know all that was ahead of him. If he had waited on the first raindrop to fall, if he had put out a fleece, if he had went for a second opinion, he would have never finished the ark in time. The flood that was coming would have swallowed him and his family.

Because of a lack of sufficient information, it can be easy to delay moving forward in faith when God speaks. While we are trying to gather enough information for us to go, the opportunity often passes by.

You may be thinking, **"Yes, I'll go, but I need more information after all, God expects us to use wisdom!"** I agree, one hundred percent! However, when and where does **'Wisdom and Faith'** part company? I am not speaking of someone having some hair brained idea, I am talking about acting upon the Word of God! It is wisdom to walk in faith, that being correct faith. As I have mentioned many times before, correct faith is in the **'Cross**

and what Jesus Christ accomplished there!' Remember, the Cross is the means and Jesus Christ is the source of all the benefits of the believer! This is the greatest step (walk) in 'Wisdom' that a person can take!

Keep in mind, the guide of your faith and wisdom is to walk in the Word; with that Word being in proper context. The Word of God will not be productive if it is taking out of context and also when faith is not in the right object. There will be times when you must look (and apply) in the Word and the principles in therein and use it with it is with its proper context to reach your goal. However it is always important to understand the context in which the Word is being used.

The next great patriarch who walked in a **'Pilgrim's Faith'** is Abraham. This story has always intrigued me concerning Abraham and his faith. He, without a doubt, is one of the greatest recorded in the **"Hall of Fame of Faith! (Hebrews 11:8).**

Abram (meaning High Father) was the son of Terah. They dwelt in the land of Ur of the Chaldees (Gen. 11:31-32; 12:1-5). It is interesting to note, that Ur of the Chaldees was possibly the most modern city of that time. They worshipped the moon god Ur. According to Jewish history (the Jewish Targum) Terah was an idol maker and Abraham worked alongside his father. It was sometime during their stay in Ur of the Chaldees that God spoke to Abram. The following has always intrigued me about this great man. Coming from a people who were embedded in the worship of a false god and how he was able to hear, and listen to the voice of God in such an atmosphere. From the time God spoke to Abram, the scriptures do not give a time frame of exactly when Abram left Ur.

When Abram left Ur of the Chaldees he and his entire family settled for a time in Haran. The time he was in Haran is not clear. We do know that he stayed there until the death of his father. We also know that he was seventy-years old when he left there. The scriptures do not tell us of any kind of encounter with God nor any revelation from God at this point and time.

> ***"Now the Lord had said unto Abram get thee out of your country, and from your kindred, and from your father's house, unto a land that I will show you." Gen. 12:1***

The promises God gave to Abram (his name was eventually changed to Abraham meaning, The Father of a multitude, is one of the most significant promises in the entirety of the Bible.

God required Abraham to surrender seven different things in his journey;

1. **He had to surrender his home land! Gen. 12:4**

2. **He had to surrender his family! Gen. 12:1**

3. **He had to surrender the plush land of Jordan! Gen. 13:5-14**

4. **He had to surrender the riches of Sodom! Gen. 14:21-24**

5. **He had to surrender himself! Gen. 15:7-9**

6. **He had to surrender Ishmael! Gen. 21:9-16**

7. **He had to surrender Isaac! Gen. 22**

Talk about a 'Leap of Faith,' ('A Pilgrim's Faith)!

In each occasion of the surrendering, God drew closer to Abraham. This is exactly what the Word does when it falls on listening ears. It creates a challenge to the hearer. It also demands action from the hearer. Every time the Word is ministered it carriers with it the measure of faith. With that faith there is the opportunity for the believer to respond!

"Faith cometh by hearing and hearing the Word"

The phrase **'Hearing the Word'** has two very distinct sides;

1. **Hearing with the ear!**

2. **Hearing with action!**

The listener not only hears the Word, but they will put to action what they heard. In other words, the hearer must do what the Word demands. This is exactly what a **'Pilgrim's Faith'** does. It hears the Word and then takes the necessary steps to do what the Word is saying! **'Now, that is a Pilgrim's Leap of Faith!**

Faith hears the Word, takes the necessary steps to do what is spoken!

I mentioned the Apostle Peter in the previous chapter. However let me expound on his story a little further. Remember when Peter and th e other disciples were in a boat and a great storm arose? It was during the storm that they noticed something or someone walking upon the water coming toward them. Fear began to grip their hearts for they thought they were seeing a spirit upon the water. It was then that Jesus spoke and said, **"Be**

of good cheer it is I be not afraid." Peter then said, **"Lord, if it be you, bid me to come unto thee on the water."** I have always been amazed at this part of the story. Jesus spoke yet Peter addressed Him as **'Lord,'** but said **'If it be you!'** I have often thought of how many times the Lord has spoken, yet, we second guess Him? Jesus responded by saying, **"Come."** It was then that Peter responded to what Jesus said, and left the safety of the boat and began to walk on the water. Just the spoken Word from Jesus aroused faith inside of Peter that caused him to do something daring!

Again, this is exactly what the Word of God does. It creates a challenge to the hearer. You may be thinking, **"Yes, but he began to sink when focusing on the storm."** You are exactly right. However, before we begin to criticize Peter, he knew who to call upon will he was sinking saying, **"Lord, save me,"** and Jesus lifted him up (just as He does any believer that will call upon Him in time of sinking (distress). When Jesus lifted Peter up, they walked back to the boat together! Peter, actually, walked on the water twice! (Matthew 14:22-33)

Just before we talk about our next person let me say, I have noticed a trap that lot of people fall into. I call it, **'The Gideon Syndrome.'** Let me explain what I mean by that statement;

An angel of the Lord appeared unto Gideon and spoke very plainly to him. The angel told Gideon that the **'Lord'** was with him. He also referred to Gideon as **'A Mighty Man of Valor!'** The angel of the Lord gave instructions to Gideon and even revealed to him how God was going to use him. (Judges 6) was not enough for Gideon, he sought a sign (Judges 6:17) to make sure this was truly an Angel of the Lord. With the conformation that this was an Angel of the Lord, Gideon proceeded to tear down the altars of Baal.

By this time you would think that Gideon was prepared for battle, but, he sought yet another sign (Judges 6:33-40). Gideon begins what I call **'testing the word of the Angel of the Lord!'** What makes this so incredible to me is, this **Angel was the pre-incarnate appearance of Jesus Christ!**

Gideon begins what I refer to as the **'Infamous Fleecing'** the reason I refer to this the way I have is because of a statement from Gideon himself. Gideon began his fleecing of God in Judges 6:36-40;

Fleece number one;

> *"Behold, I will put a fleece of wool in the floor; and if the dew be on the fleece only, and it be dry upon all the earth beside, then shall I know that you will save Israel by my hand, as You have said."*

> *"And it was so: for he rose up early on the morrow, and thrust the fleece together, a bowl full of water." Judges 6:37-38*

Gideon wasn't finished. His next statement proves that he was still hesitant to go forward. **Fleece number 2;**

> *"And Gideon said unto God, Let not your anger be hot against me, I will speak this once: let me prove I pray you, but this once with the fleece; let it now be dry only upon the fleece, and upon the ground let there be dew."*

"And God did so that night: for it was dry upon the fleece only, and there was dew on all the ground." Judges 6:39-40

I do not for a moment believe that Gideon did this fleecing trying to find the will of God. With all of the previous information, it is evident he knew what God called him to do. I think Gideon was looking for a security blanket!

Keeping these two tests in mind Williams says; "The double test with the fleece made plain to Gideon that God could withhold and grant blessing. He could bless Gideon, and no one else; and, on the other hand, He could bless everybody else, and not Gideon. Rahab and Jericho illustrates the one action and Nineveh and Jonah the other"

After the fleecing, God reduced Gideon's army from thirty-two thousand to a measly three hundred men to defeat the Midianites. Whatever Gideon's intent was, he was assured that it would take God going before him to win the battle!

As great a story as this is, the believer today has no reason to put out fleeces. Our ultimate victory is in the **'Finished Work of Jesus Christ at Calvary**! This is all of the evidence we need to secure our walk of victory! (Romans 6) It is unfruitful to be fleecing (testing) God for what He has already supplied. Again, that supply come from the **'Cross which is the means and Jesus Christ who is the source for everything you and I will need in life!**

If you are living a life of fleecing, you are missing out (or delaying) on some of the greatest blessings that God has supplied! **"But brother Baldock, I have put out fleeces and they work!"** That may very well be true. However, faith will reach out and grab the promise while fleecing is still trying to figure it out! Fleecing also gives the enemy (Satan) room to work on and even deceive the believer. It is walking and living in faith that pleases God! (Heb. 11:6) After all, we are talking about living in an **'Adventurous Faith!' A Pilgrim's Faith! A Faith blazing a trail, and does not look back. This kind of faith has the ability to see what the natural eye can't. This faith has as its object what Jesus Christ accomplished at Calvary!**

<u>This Faith Goes Before You Know!</u>

CHAPTER 5

A Pilgrim's Faith is a Visionary Faith

A **'Visionary,'** according to Random House Webster's College Dictionary, is defined as; a person whose ideas, or projects, are impractical (but not impossible); a dreamer, or one who is likely to see visions. A **'Vision'** is the act or power of imaginations; a supernatural appearance that conveys revelation.

From the above definitions, we are able to determine that a **'visionary'** is someone who is able to see beyond the impossible. For the believer, it is the ability to see beyond their current situations and see the promises of God! They have the ability to embrace them, even when they are far off. To be a visionary, one must not settle for where they are at, nor for what they possess. A **'visionary'** is always looking and desiring better!

> *"These all died in faith not having received the promises, but, having seen them far off, and were persuaded of them, and embraced them, and confessed that they were strangers and pilgrim's on the earth." Heb. 11:13*

The writer of Hebrews (which I believe to be the Apostle Paul) is referring to men .i.e the **'patriarchs'** of old such as, Abel, Enoch, Noah, Abraham, Isaac, Jacob, Moses, and many others. They all looked toward the promised Messiah, Jesus Christ and what He would accomplish at Calvary. While they looked forward to the promises, the believer of today must look back at the **'Cross and the Finished Works of Jesus Christ!** Let's examine the tenacity of faith of those before us!

They Saw The Promises!

I think it is interesting to note, even though the promises were afar off, they through the eyes of faith, could see them! They had to look beyond their current situations and circumstances in order to accomplish their goal!

Too often, we allow our past and present to be so clouded with doubt and fear, that we cannot see afar off. I am sure that there have been times while driving in an intense fog, where you could barely see the road in front of you. I have found myself in this very situation. I have been driving in a fog that was so dense that I could barely see the front of my car. When those times have happened, I would look for something to guide my path, like the middle yellow line, or the white line on the side of the road. There have been times when I was driving on a road that had neither yellow lines in the middle, nor white lines on the side. Yet, I continued driving, with my destination in my mind's eye. This is exactly what it is like, when we allow the path we are traveling to become clouded.

When you read and study about the patriarch's of faith, you will discover that there were times when the path they were on seemed so clouded. Yet, they continued their trek of faith; seeing (by faith) what God had promised and keeping it in front of them.

This reminds me of a song that contains the phrase, **"I see sunshine on a cloudy day."** Several years ago, I was traveling to Los Angeles, California. I boarded a small plane in Indianapolis. It was a cloudy, rainy day. Due to the storms the small plane that carrying us to Chicago, for a connecting flight was rough. When we landed in Chicago, it was still raining. From there, I boarded a plan going to Los Angeles. On the take off, the plane began to climb higher and higher. After reaching heights that the smaller could not reach, something amazing happened! As I looked out the window, to my surprise, the sun was shining! I learned a great lesson that day. It really doesn't matter what is going on around us. It does not, nor can it, nullify the promises of God! There is always **'sunshine on a rainy day!'**

The mistake so many believers often make, is, settling for the clouds without the promise. They become satisfied in their comfort zone and decide to live there. The apostle Paul addressed this very issue;

> *"Not that I speak in respect of want: for I have learned, in whatsoever state I am, therewith to be content." Phil. 4:11*

Did you notice, Paul said, he had **'learned'** to be **'content,'** no matter the state or conditions around him? First notice, Paul said he" **learned!'** The one who taught this great apostle was the Holy Spirit. It was the Holy Spirit who took Paul through each adventure teaching and revealing to him greatness the Word! (See 2 Cor. 11:16-33; 12:1-10). This is one word that every believer needs to engage in, **'Learning!'**

The word **'content,'** needs further clarification. To the surprise of many, it does not mean, **'to be satisfied,'** neither does it mean the lack of desire for something better. In this instance, the word, **'content,'** is to be completely detached from surrounding circumstances. In other words, this great Apostle was saying, **'I have learned to live in need; I have learned to be abased (brought to the lowest point); I have learned to abound (have an overabundance.'** However, none of these situations took my eyes off of what God had promised! (Phil. 4:12). He never allowed any circumstances, no matter how small or great, to overcome him!

Paul discovered the greatness of God's grace, which enabled him to look beyond his past and current situations, and take hold of what Jesus Christ accomplished at Calvary! (2 Cor. 12:1-10). Without any doubt, Paul lived in a pilgrim kind of faith! He truly was a **'trailblazer with a visionary faith.'**

Think of the great patriarch, Abraham (we will discuss him in greater depth in another chapter). He left his country and family (although he Lot) not knowing exactly where he was going. All he knew was that God spoke and told him to go to a place He (God) had for him, and he went.

God has designed a place for you! And, it is better than where you are presently! You may be thinking, "I don't need anything else, I am perfectly fine where I am." **However, God has got even greater things in store for you!** I am not talking, necessarily about you physical place, but rather, more importantly your spiritual place! There is always room for improvement! I am convinced, no matter your present spiritual condition, God has higher ground for you!

<u>You Must Desire Better!</u>

A Visionary faith has the ability to see the invisible, obtain the unobtainable, touch the untouchable, make real the unreal, and make possible the impossible! Now is you time to, **"Go For It!'**

> *"But now they desire a better country, that is a heavenly:" Heb. 11:16a*

For any of the previous statements to take place, you must desire better. What I mean by desiring something better, is to continually progress, grow and mature in Christ. So many of the modern day church have fallen prey to just being comfortable. They find a comfortable place, and stay there! However, the position of every believer should be to reach a goal of their spiritual condition, to meet there spiritual position!

To keep progressing in the things that Jesus Christ has provided! So, don't just sit there and settle for what you have, when better (progress) is before you! It is the desire of **'better'** that has given us the many conveniences that we enjoy today. Thank God for the microwave oven, the automatic dishwasher, the automatic washer and dryer, the automobile, the cell phone, etc. All of these amenities are the result of someone desiring something better, and refusing to settle, in their particular place.

To desire something better begins with the ability to see beyond where you are, and, being restrained by what you see physically. As we have mentioned before, the patriarchs, such as, Abraham, Isaac, Jacob and many others, were able to see beyond where they were at and take hold of what God had promised! They had **'visionary faith!'**

Another key to things getting better is the ability to see them getting better. When I think of someone in this kind of condition mind goes to Joseph, and all that he endured before he became the viceroy of Egypt. He kept his faith, when his brothers betrayed him. He kept his faith, when he was sold into slavery. He kept his faith, when Potiphar's wife lied on him. He kept his faith, while being imprisoned, and through the chief butler not remembering him. In the end, Joseph became what God intended. His greatest request was that his bones be removed from Egypt, and carried into the land of promise. What a **'visionary!'** He was able to look far ahead, and see things getting better for all of Israel!

Avoid the trap of stinking thinking that says, **'things will never change for the better!' 'And if they ever do change, it will probably be for the worse!'** Begin to see yourself as a victory, not a victim! It is time to get out and go! It is time for you to remove yourself from a losing attitude, and see yourself as a winner in Jesus Christ! Jesus Christ paid the cost to bring you out!

The scriptures proclaim that you, the believer, are not the tail but you are the head! You are not under but you are above! **(Deut. 28:1-13; Eph. 1:20-23).** You are more than a conqueror; you can do all things through Christ Jesus; you do have the mind of Christ; you have not been given the spirit of fear, but of love, power, and the soundness of mind; the gates of Hell cannot prevail against you, because **'You are a child of God!'** Now, begin to receive, and walk in what the Word of God declares about you! And, begin to see things getting better!

<u>You Must Put Your Current Situation Behind You!</u>

In order for things to get better, it will be imperative for you to remove yourself from your current situation. Before you get to happy, that this is a way out a commitment gone bad, such as a marriage, think again. However, there will be times when you (the believer) must separate (detach) yourself from anything that is keeping you from progressing in the kingdom of God. In my personal experience, that separation began my mind. In other words, my mind set had to change. The apostle Paul said, He forgot those things that were behind him and continued to reach for those things ahead of him. (Phil.3:13).

There possible could be geographical change needed. However, keep in mind, a geographical change will not help if you stay in same frame of mind that has held you down.

Think of it for a moment about our forefathers. They had to leave their situation to go after something better. Their desire was for something better than what they were in. They we falling prey to oppression and there had to be a move. Their worship to God was being suppressed. So much so, that something had to give. Things had to get better.

They began to desire a better country, a place where they could excel in the Word of God. In order for their desires to come to pass, they had to remove themselves from the situations they were facing. They boarded ships and set sail for a better country. This reminds me of a stanza in a poem, by Helen Wheeler Wilcox, where she makes this statement;

> *"It is the setting of the sail, and not the gail,*
> *that determines the course of the ship"*

It is the setting of your desire for the promises of God that will determine the course of your life. When you set your desires on the will of God, and give the Holy Spirit the latitude to give direction, it will cause you to travel on the course that God has for you!

> *"Delight thyself also in the Lord; an He shall*
> *give you the desires of thine heart." Psalm 37:4*

The word, *'delight,* comes with the idea of the believer becoming soft and pliable in the hands of God. In other words, He (God) is the potter and the believer is the clay. When the believer is put in this place (upon the potters-wheel) his/her desires of the flesh are left behind then the desire for the things of God come to the forefront. This will create a new path to travel!

***"The steps of a good man are ordered by the
Lord: and he delighteth in his way" Psalm 37:23***

Within the previous passage of scripture, a great truth is revealed. First, once your desires change from a fleshly lust to a spiritual desire, God will begin to fill them. Secondly, once all your faith and trust is in Jesus Christ, and what He accomplished at Calvary, He begins to order your steps and take care of you! He will never forsake you! Neither will he allow you to be in want! (Psalm. 23)

God has a plan for you to leave your comfort zone (relying on self). Oftentimes to accomplish such a task, your comfort zone (your nest) will begin to become uncomfortable. It will become like the mother eagle, when she begins to stir he nest. She will begin to remove what made the nest comfortable. This will cause her young to get up onto the side of the nest. Now, she is going begin to teach and train them to fly in the heavens, as they were created to do. She will stretch forth her mighty wing ack. and call for them to come and settle on her back. While she is soaring, she will shake them from her back, in an attempt to encourage them to fly. They will begin tumbling to the earth, trying to fly. While they are yet unable to fly, she will then fly downward and catch them. This process will continue until her young begins to fly. There will be times when your nest will no longer be comfortable, that possible is God saying, **'It is time to soar!'**

You may be facing some uncomfortable situations in your current place, instead of trying to make it comfortable. What is keeping you from asking God to reveal to you what He is trying to teach you? Then, you may see your situation as a sign from God desiring better for you, and is trying to get you to see it! You were not created to stay safely nestled within a nest. God has a place for you, and you can arrive there when you begin to desire better! You were created to be above all principalities, and power, and might, and dominion, and every name that is named, not only in this world, but also in that which is to come! **(Eph. 1:21).** You were made to sit in heavenly places together with Christ **(Eph. 2:6)!**

You were not called of God to remain imprisoned within yourself. He has called you to walk in the power of His anointing! For this to happen, you must see beyond where you are now!

Sometimes, making up your mind to leave your current situation can be difficult. But, while you are in that situation, you need to take time to examine it from every angle. First and foremost examine it spiritually see if moving will make things better. Don't make a move just to be moving. Remember, no matter where you go, you cannot run from a problem! Problems will follow you if they are not faced and taken care of. The move I am referring to (previously mentioned) has to be a God move!

I want to take a moment and share with you four men who found themselves in a difficult situation. You will find these men sitting outside of the city of Samaria. These men were stricken with the dreaded disease of leprosy. Samaria was surrounded by the Syrian army. They did not have any way of getting food into the city. The people within were starving so badly, two women agreed to boil their sons to eat. The first woman boiled her son, and they ate. The net day, the second woman refused to boil her son. The city was in chaos. They were even selling doves dung to fill their starvation. Something had to be done! (2 Kings

6:24-33; 7:1-5) When you read the entire story, you will find that God had provisions for them, He was waiting on someone to make a move! The four lepers looked at one another and said;

> ***"Why sit we here until we die?" If we say, We will enter into the city, then the famine is in the city, and we shall die there: and if we sit here, we die also. Now therefore come, and let us fall unto the host of the Syrians: if they save us alive we shall live; And if they kill us, we shall but die."***
> ***2 Kings 7:3b-4***

They decided to make a move, not realizing their move would change not only their situation but the entire city would change! When they moved forwards, toward the Syrians, God created a great noise of chariots and horses! The thundering sound caused the Syrians to run from their camp. They left all of their sustenance behind. When the four lepers arrived there, they found plenty to Eat! They ended up sharing the spoils within the entire city! What a move!

When you look at all that is going on around you take a moment, and think; you just may be in the need of making a move! Someone, somewhere, may be waiting your move! Moving forward could be the very thing that will cause God's supplies to come to you abundantly. Keep in mind, I am talking more about spiritual moves than a geographical move, or a move to a different church, unless the church you are attending is dying or already dead, then by all means, make a move!

I have witnessed people who continue to sit in dead places, dead churches, because their family has attended that place for years.

They have become like a fruit that is dying on the branch, but still will not make a make a move! I have also seen those who were stuck waist deep in tradition and religion. And, they also refuse to make a move!

It is sad to think that all it takes is one move to change everything around you, and people will still not move, because of the fear of change. They have become satisfied where they are at and have no desire for things to change or get better. Some even go to the extreme, and believe, if things would change, it would more than likely be worse. Another frame of mind that keeps some down is, things are as good as they are going to get, right where they are. However, if they could get a **'pilgrim's mentality,'** they would always be looking for things to change for the better! It is called, **'progressing, growing and maturing in Jesus Christ!'**

Things will begin to look better when a person begins to look in the right places! This is what makes the **'spirit of a pilgrim,'** so exciting! They will look n every direction, in an attempt to find the right place; that is, the place where the **'blessings of God are flowing!'**

Jesus made a tremendous statement when He said; *"For where your treasure is, there will your heart be also." Matt.6:21*

I have heard that statement quoted, since I was a child, and I had never stopped to think about how true it really is! Let's take a moment and examine what Jesus said. **1. Your heart is your treasure chest. 2. What finds its way into your heart is the direct result of what you continue to dwell on! 3. What you**

dwell on becomes your treasure! This is one reason why, as a believer, one should dwell on heavenly things!

> *"While we look not at the things which are seen, but at the things which are not seen; for the things which are seen are temporal: but the things which are seen are eternal." 2. Cor. 4:18*

The pilgrims of faith set their sight on the heavenly things;

> *"But they desire a better country, that is a heavenly wherefore God is not ashamed to be called their God: for He hath prepared for them a city." Hebrews 11:16*

Not only should we be thankful for all of the promises of God, but we also should be thankful for the revelation of these great promises! They began in the heavenly and have come down from the **'throne of God!'** Now, we can be partakers of them through the **'Cross and the finished work of Jesus Christ!'**

> *"If ye be risen with Christ, seek those things which are above, where Christ sitteth on the right hand of God.!"*

> *"Set your affections on the things above, not on things on the earth." Col. 3:1-2o be*

The above passage of scripture tells us where, and what the believer is to be seeking, with all of their affections! This takes us on an adventure that leads to a life of **'Victory!'**

Remember, where your treasure is, that is where your heart will be! It will take a **'visionary mentality'** to see what Jesus Christ accomplished for us, and to see all that is in **'God's treasure chest of blessings!' Why don't you go ahead, and take that step forward, and walk down that trail that has been blazed for you! You will be amazed at what you will discover!**

Let me leave this chapter with a great quote from one of if not the best college basketball coaches of all time;

> **Things will turn out the best for the people**
> **who make the best of the way things turn out!"**
> **Coach John Wooden**

What a great quote! Let me say, "For things to turn out the best, one must take Jesus Christ as their personal Lord and Savior!

CHAPTER 6

Pilgrims Are Persuaded of the Promises!

There are times when it may seem that the promises of God are totally out of reach. Have you ever found yourself waiting for a promise and it is getting down to the last minute, and you wonder, "Where is God?" There may even be times when the waiting seems to be so long that you grow impatient and, before long, frustration sets in. You begin to think that you may have to help God out with this one, so, what is a person to do in a time like this to keep from getting frustrated? I believe the key is to remain focused on what God has promised in His Word and, to keep a mental picture of the manifestation of that promise!

The patriarchs of old believed that the promises of God were true and they were persuaded of them. They kept their minds and faith on the land of promise that was before them. They believed in the ability of God to provide. They knew that they would one day walk in what God had promised!

> *"These all died in the faith not having received the promises, but having seen them afar off, and were persuaded of them, and embraced them, and confessed that they were strangers and pilgrims in the earth." Heb. 11:13*

The phrase, *"These all died in faith"* of course we know that during this time, Enoch did not see death, but the stress here is not laid upon the death of those believers, but upon their having retained their faith through life.— Matthew Henry— Bloomfield from Magee.

The Greek text reads, *"According to Faith"* meaning they died under the regime of faith, and of sight (Vincent) it is also important to notice what it is saying. First, let's look at what it is not saying. It does not say, *"By faith these all died."* But it does say, *"These all died in faith"* which is the same as saying, *"These all died in accordance to faith."* This simply means that faith was how they lived. Faith was the very foundation of their walk with God. There should not be any difference in the walk of the Christian today. We should have as our foundation faith in what Jesus Christ done at Calvary! Another of saying this would be, *"They looked toward the cross while the believer today is to look back at the cross!"*

The phrase, *"not having received the promises"* This statement is in twofold. 1. They did not come into possession of the Land of Canaan 2. Jesus Christ did not come in their lifetime. However, the next phrase e\seals their faith. *"But having seen them afar off"* Although there were promises which they never experienced they never wavered in their faith. They kept those promises in front of them consistently.

The phrase *"and were persuaded of them"* They were persuaded that what God had said was true and that he would bring them to pass. This phrase also carries with it the idea that the patriarchs were so persuaded of that which God revealed that they gladly exchange what they could see for which they could not see!

The phrase *"and embraced "* states the fact that even though they could not see with their natural eyesight, yet, they claimed and took hold of what God promised. They **'embraced'** the promises, even though, they were afar off! There is a lesson here for the church of today to take hold of. The beginning of the manifestation of the promise is to first see them and then speak them. Everything that the believer will ever need is in the **'cross!'** (Luke 9:23) It is time to *'embrace' 'the finished work of Jesus Christ!* (Heb. 12:1-2)

The phrase *"and confessed that they were strangers and pilgrims on earth."* This is a confession that should be coming from the mouth of every true Christian. Jesus said, *"We are not of this world" (John 15:19; 17:14-25) "His kingdom is not in (of) this world (John 18:36).*

A pilgrim's faith remains persuaded of the promises of God. They may not seem them in the physical, but they still remain persuaded of them. When I think of someone be persuaded of what God spoke, I think of Abraham. Abraham is a great example of a person being persuaded of the promises of God!

> *"He (Abraham) staggered not at the promises of God through unbelief; but was strong in faith, giving glory to God;"*

"And being fully persuaded that, what God had promised He was able also to perform." Romans 4:20-21

The phrase, *"being fully persuaded,"* is from the Greek word, *'Pierophoria,'* this is a compound word; first *"pieres"* meaning; full; the word *'phoreo,'* meaning; to fill. Together, it means, to fulfill, thoroughly accomplish, to be fulfilled, being established, being brought to an end and completed, reaching its goal, to be proved fully.

Abraham was so convinced (persuaded) of the promises of God, that he was able to see, by faith, the finished and completed plan (promise). For twenty-five years in the making, with his body dead (unable to produce children), and the deadness of Sarah's womb, he still was persuaded of what God had promised.

Webster's dictionary defines **'Persuaded'** as; to prevail on (a person) to do something, as by advising or urging; to induce to believe, to convince.

The above definitions, confirms the kind of faith that says, **"We will reach our goal!"** This is exactly the kind of faith that blazes a trail! It is a mindset that nothing and I mean nothing, can nor will rattle me nor cause me to waver in what I believe (James 1:6)! Take thought of the following:

One ship drives east
And another drives west
With the selfsame winds that blow
Tis the set of the sails and not the gales
Which tells us the way to go

**Like the winds of the sea
Tis the set of the soul
That decides its goal
And not the calm or the strife!
Helen Wheeler Wilcox**

The preceding poem is one of my all-time favorites. It is extraordinary how the setting of the soul to a particular goal can bring a calming effect! That is what a **"pilgrim's faith"** brings to the believer! Even when there is chaos surrounding your (our) journey, there is little, or no concern, when walking in true faith! This is so true when our eyes of faith are upon the goal (the promises of God) that are set before us!

So, to persuade is to influence someone's thoughts or actions. It implies the action of wining over a person to a certain course of action, or belief. Being persuaded is a powerful force that drives a person to a particular place, thing, or belief! It also creates a focus that will take the mind off of surrounding distractions, as we have seen the evidence in the life of Abraham. He was **'fully persuaded"** in his walk of faith that when God promised him a son, he waited for twenty-five years for the manifestation!

It is important to take notice, when Abraham was against *'hope,'* he yet believed in hope! When it appeared, by all external things, that the promise of God had vanished, he yet believed! This in itself should be of great encouragement to every believer, who is yet to see the manifestation of the (a) promise; to hold on tight, never wavering, being fully persuaded, while still waiting! Never give up, nor let go, no matter what is going on around you!

The second thing to take into consideration, concerning Abraham and his walk of faith, is that he was not weak in his faith!

> *"And being not weak in faith he considered not his own body now dead, when he was about one hundred years old, neither yet the deadness of Sarah's womb" Romans 4:19*

I am convinced that the faith given to you and I, is no less than the faith give to Abraham, and it is well able to bring to pass the manifestation of the promises of God! However, it is vital for every believer to remain strong in their faith, never wavering!

> *"But let him ask in faith, nothing wavering. For he that wavereth is like the wav of the sea driven with the wind and tossed."*

> *"For let not that man think that he shall receive any thing of the Lord."*

> *"A double minded man is unstable in all his ways." James 1:6-8*

Did you notice in the above passage of scripture that is was not the wavering of faith, but rather the person wavering in their faith? This is a clear indication that while walking in faith the believer must remained focused on the Word!

True faith, and by that I mean a faith having the right object in its sight, will never let go nor let you down! Faith will never fail!

It is when we lose sight of the **"cross and the finished work of Jesus Christ,"** that we lose strength, which creates wavering through our weakness. It wasn't that Abraham had stronger faith than you or I, but that Abraham was strong in his faith! It was certainly **"A pilgrim's faith"** that allowed this great patriarch to walk the road where nobody had traveled before! It was Abraham who refused to waver, while God was leading him down this great walk of faith!

The third thing to take in consideration, concerning Abraham's walk of faith is that he did not allow his surroundings to dictate his walk. When he and Sarah had passed the age of physical ability to produce children, Abraham refused to let go of the promise! Too often, we put limitations on God and remove ourselves from the promise! It is important to identify the distractions, remove them, and continue to hold onto what God has said. You may be asking, **"How can I remove the distractions?"** You can remove them by not allowing them to dictate how you feel on the inside, and also by not focusing on what is surrounding you!

The fourth thing I want you to notice, concerning Abraham, is that **"he did not Stagger at the promises of God through unbelief!"** He refused to become overwhelmed with the promise or with his and Sarah's age.

The word, **'stagger,'** is from the Greek word, **"Diakrino."** This is a compound word; *"dia"* denoting separation, and *"krino"* meaning to distinguish, to decide. In Romans 4:20, it is to doubt and to be distinguished, or divided in one's mind.

This is exactly what Abraham refused to do! This reveals Abraham's spiritual and mental attitude! He did not allow his mind to be divided when it came to what God had spoken to him. As we noted earlier, *"A double minded man is unstable in all his ways." James 1:8.* This truly describes how determined a **'pilgrim's faith'** really is!

Another ingredient found in a **'pilgrim's faith'** and was evident with the character of Abraham is **'persistence.'** Persistence is the attitude that says, *"I refuse to give in, I will remain steadfast and determined."* I am convinced that persistence has a twin brother named **'patience.'** This set of twins can be one of the greatest assets of the believer, especially when walking in a **'pilgrim's faith!'**

The loss of either of these twins can, and often does, create a loss of hope. The loss of hope for a pilgrim can be devastating! The faith of a pilgrim says, **"It may take awhile, and I may go through some difficult times. However, I will make it through to reach my goal!"**

Your amount of persuasion of what God has promised will be found in your amount of determination and patience! When the word, patience, is mentioned, the person I most often think of is Job. His patience has been the centerpiece of many Christian conversations. He stood through many trials, and tests, and at the end, he was blessed even more than at the beginning!

My grandmother, who went on to be with the Lord in October of 1971, used the following phrase all the time. She would say, **"The Proof is in the Pudding!"** Thanks grandma, that phrase has rang true in my walk with God!

Well, all through the scriptures, there is overwhelming proof that when walking in faith, the twin brothers of **"Determination and Patience"** has a great payday! They are the ingredients that help bring about the reaching of the goal that is before every believer!

I have no idea where you stand, in your current situation while waiting on the promises of God. However, I want to encourage you to continue to hold on with the tenacity of faith. When it comes to the believer of today, they (we) must have the same tenacity of faith! We must begin to walk in the benefits (provisions) of the **"Finished Work of Jesus Christ at Calvary!"**

Whatever it is that you may be facing and or going through, remember the following;

"This too shall pass!"
"Your current situation is but for a season!"
"You are at the brink of an outbreak!"
"The manifestation of the (your) promise
and your goal, is just around the corner!"
"Keep your focus on Jesus Christ" Hebrews 12:2

<u>Continue too Build Up Yourself</u>

<u>And Become Strong In The Faith!</u>

"But ye, beloved, (every born again believer)
building up (doing those thing that will make
you and keep you strong) yourselves on your
most holy faith (your faith in the cross and what
Jesus Christ accomplished there is your Holy

foundation0 praying in the Holy Ghost." (the Holy Ghost not only must be the director (Ro 6) and the leader (Ro.8) of your life. He must also take the leadership in your prayer life Ro. 8:25-27!) Jude 20 Emphasis are mine

CHAPTER 7

A Pilgrim's Faith 'Embraces the Promises'

"These all died in (according to) faith, not
having received the promises, but having seen
them afar off, and were persuaded of them,
and embraced them, and confessed that they
were strangers and pilgrims on earth"
Hebrews 11:13

We touched on this passage of scripture in the previous chapter, however it bares repeating To **'embrace'** the promises of God are one of the most important steps, in receiving what God has spoken! This is especially true, when the promises, are yet **'afar of.'** (Heb. 11:13).

The word, **'embrace,'** is from the Greek word, **'aspazomia,'** meaning; to welcome, to greet.

The patriarchs of old, **'embraced'** (welcomed and greeted) the promises, while they were yet unseen. These great and precious promises, by faith, became a vital part of their living. Their everyday living was filled with hope and dreams, and their futures were placed in what God had promised. This was not only true for the **pilgrims of faith,** it must also be true for every believer today!

It is important to be aware that the **'embracing'** of the promises was done by faith, before ever seeing the manifestation!

For the believers today, nothing has changed! The possession of all that God has promised can only come by **'welcoming, and greeting,'** and this is only done by faith!

The one difference between the patriarchs and today's believer is that the patriarchs looked toward the Messiah and what He would accomplish on the cross. Today's believer must look back at the **'cross and the finished work of Jesus Christ.' John 19:30!** Everything, and I mean everything, the believer will ever need comes through the **'cross,'** which is the means, and through, **'Jesus Christ,'** who is the source.

> *"And He said to them all, if any man will come after Me, let him deny himself, and take up his cross daily and follow Me." Luke 9:23*

Let's take a closer look as to what Jesus was saying to the elders and chief priests: As we get started, it is important to establish the subject in which Jesus was referring to, which is any person who is seeking salvation. And then, he follows with the criteria for discipleship.

The phrase; ***"If any man come after me,"*** again, this denotes any person who is seeking salvation; realizing that the only way to the Father is through Jesus Christ. It also denotes anyone seeking a better life i.e. **'a newness of life!'**

The phrase; **'let him,'** is not a suggestion or a request, but rather a command. This is stated, and written grammatically, in aorist imperative; which is a command for doing something in the future! That is a simple act. It is written in the future, because Jesus had yet to go to Calvary as the supreme sacrifice. It is also in the passive voice; representing the subject (anyone coming to Jesus Christ, and that for salvation) as receiving the benefits for the action, i.e. **'let and or to let.'**

The phrase; ***'deny himself,'*** is one of great importance and has been misunderstood and misrepresented in a huge way. The word is from the Greek word, ***'aparneomia'*** meaning; to remove oneself, refuse, deny, disown. This word occurs only once and is a personal objective; meaning, to decline or withdraw from fellowship with (the flesh) anyone. This is not asceticism, a many may think. It has been taught and preached that in order to deny oneself it takes severe self-discipline, and to avoid all forms of indulgence; typically for religious reasons. For some examples;

I can remember in the early 1950's, actually 1956, when I received Jesus Christ as my Lord and Savior. There were many who preached against board games with dice, any kind of card games and especially mixed bathing! Back, in 1971 when I began in the ministry, self-denial was taught excessively. Being a Christian meant being separated from amusement parks movies, and as I mentioned before, God forbid that you would play a game of cards. The women were supposed to wear dresses that came from their neck to their ankles, and the often could not wear open toed shoes. They were not allowed to cut their hair, and the men were not supposed to allow their hair to touch their ears. Those in ministry had to wear white long sleeve shirts, and their suits were normally grey, black or brown. Depending on what part of the country you were in, some in ministry could not wear a neck tie. There was no swimming and television was a no, no!

I think by now (I hope) you are getting the idea. I admit that some of these things were extreme, and it these rules were really determined by the mot ministry one sat under. As good as these intentions might have been this is not what Jesus was referring to.

The correct meaning of the term, **'deny oneself,'** is for the believer to deny living and walking within their own ability, self-will, (will power), and strength, depending totally on Jesus Christ. As a believer, we must stop trying to live for Jesus Christ in our own fleshly ability and with our own understanding. When the believer follows the instruction that Jesus gave, there will be a change of lifestyle. However, it is a change on the inside and works its way to the outside!

> *"I beseech you therefore, brethren, by the mercies of God, that ye present (put yourself in the position of opportunity) your bodies a living sacrifice (a life of separation), holy, acceptable unto God, which is your reasonable service."*

> *"And be not conformed (fashioned after) to this world: but be ye transformed by the renewing of your mind, that ye may prove what is that good, acceptable, and perfect will of God (the proving of the will of God is manifested when change takes place)" Romans 12:1-2 Emphasis mine*

Please understand, the following will never come to pass without adhering to verse 1

The word, *'conformed'* is from the Greek word, *'suschematizo.''* This is a compound word; *'sun'* meaning; together with, and *'schematize'* meaning; fashion. Do not fall in with the external and fleeting fashions of this age, nor be not fashioned to them. But rather, undergo a deep inner change. The change on the inside will be evident on the outside!

The word, *'transformed,'* is from the Greek word, *'metamorphoo' and 'metamorphoomai.'* The word, *'meta'* is denoting a change of condition, and *'morphoo'* meaning, to form. This comes with the idea of a transformation, referring to an invisible process in Christians (the believer), which begins upon a new birth, and continues through their life with Christ, in this present age. It is a change of **'quality,'** not of, **'quantity!'** It involves a **'qualitative'** change for a new use. It is to be **'transformed' i.e. 'transformation'** into God's completed work. In 2 Corinthians 3:16-18, the word in verse 18, **'changed'** is used. And this word is from the same Greek word as **'transformation,'** used in Romans 12:2. Again, this change, which begins on the inside, will be manifested (seen) on the outside!

"Therefore if any man be in Christ, he is a new creature: old things are passed away; behold, all things are become new." 2 Cor. 5:17

In the above scripture, it is speaking of a renewal or a refreshing. This new creation is not the old man reworked, but rather a transformed i.e. changed man! God does not have a rehab program. When God enters in, a qualitative change takes place; meaning you are a new creation; a new creature!

The example I used earlier, concerning how many tried **'denying'** themselves, by doing or doing external things, will never make a new creature. The change within the believer is done totally through being **'born again' (John 3:1-7)** this is a work of sanctification and can only be done by the Holy Spirit!

There is just no other way that one can accomplish being a new creation by the means of the flesh (our works)!

The phrase, ***'take up his cross'*** is two-fold

1. **Take up;** is a command for doing something in the future. I said earlier, it was future, because Jesus Christ had yet to be crucified (go to the cross) However, for the believer today, it is in the **'now!** It is denoting a simple action, and or aim. This is something that every believer must do themselves, nobody can do it for you, this is accomplished through the strength and power of the Holy Spirit!

2. **His Cross;** it is important to understand **'what cross,'** is to be taken up. It is the cross of the subject, i.e. the

believer! Those who come to Christ must take up their cross!

The 'cross' has two very important elements;

A. Death side-suffering

B. The victory side

Most of the time when the phrase *'take up his cross'* is used, the first thing thought of is death, burden and carrying a heavy load in this life! They forget about the **'victory'** that was accomplished there! The word **'cross'** is from the Greek word, *'stauros,'* meaning to stand. It symbolizes the suffering of (with) Jesus Christ, which is to die with Him! But also, this means to live with Him (Romans 6:2-6)!

The apostle Paul said it this way;

> *"That I may know him, (refers to an understanding of what Jesus Christ accomplished at Calvary), and the power of His resurrection, (refers to the benefits of His resurrection and the living in the newness of life) see Roman 6:3-6, and the fellowship of His suffering (that is to put all of ones faith and trust in what He accomplished at the cross, and walking in the benefits He has provided for every believer) Being made conformable unto His death (whatever He put to death, the believer must put to death, this is the only way to salvation)! Phil 3:10 Emphasis mine*

To take his (our) cross is the beginning of living in the benefits of the **'cross'** and the **'finished work of Jesus' (John 19:30)**! From this point forward, the believer is to look exclusively to the **'cross'** which is the **'means,'** and to **'Jesus Christ who is the source'** of all the believer will ever have need of!

Please understand, I am not saying we will never hard times. There is a fight of faith to stay the course. However, Jesus Christ has made a way for the believer to walk in victory!

With the above information, it bears a question, "Why would Jesus require the believer to take up a cross of such an unbearable heavy burden, when he said?"

> *"Come unto me, all ye that labor and are heavy laden and I will give you rest."*
>
> *"Take: for my yoke upon you, learn of me; for I am meek and lowly in heart: ye shall find rest for your souls."*
>
> *"For my yoke is easy, and my burden is light."*
> *Matt. 11:28-30*
>
> *"The thief cometh not, but for to steal, and to kill, and to destroy: I am come that they might have life, and that they have it more abundantly."*
> *John 10:10*
>
> *"In this world, ye shall have tribulation, but be of good cheer I have overcome the world." John 16:33b*

This certainly does not sound like Jesus went to the **'cross'** to leave the believer with a defeated life! On the contrary, He has made it possible for every believer to live an overcoming victorious life! That certainly does not mean a life that is trouble free, but a life of victory over the cares of this life! Paul said;

> ***"I am crucified with Christ (what Christ put to death is dead in me) nevertheless I live; yet not I, but Christ liveth in me: (what Christ brought to life is alive in me) and the life that I now live in the flesh I live by the faith of the Son of God (I now live by the faithfulness of Jesus Christ and by what He accomplished at the cross) who loved me and gave Himself for me. (Jesus Christ gave of Himself and became the supreme sacrifice to bring everlasting life to whomsoever)! Gal. 2:20 Emphasis mine***

The apostle Paul was living the life found in Romans Chapters 6 and 8. This brings us to **'The Cross and Discipleship.'**

1. **The believer reckons and counts himself crucified with Christ! Romans 6:11; Galatians 2:20; 5:24**

2. **The believer reckons and counts himself dead to sin once and always! Romans 6:5-9; Romans 8**

3. **The believer reckons himself alive in Christ! Romans 6:11; 1 Peter 4:2**

4. **The believer does not let (allow) the sin nature to reign and rule in their body, nor do they yield the parts of the body to sin (the sin nature) as an**

instrument of wickedness! Romans 6:12-13; 8:13; Colossians 3:5

5. **The believer yields himself to Jesus Christ! Romans 6:13b; 12:1-21; 13:14**

6. **The believer yields his body members as an instrument of righteousness! Romans 6:1w3c; Romans 8; Galatians 5:16**

7. **The believer mortifies the deeds of this body! Romans 8:13**

The command **'take up his cross'** is extremely important! It is given with the idea that one is to look to the **'Cross daily.'** This also comes with the idea of renewing your faith and mind on a daily basis. It is to be reminded, daily, of what Jesus Christ accomplished at the Cross! It is also to walk daily in the benefits of all that Jesus Christ accomplished for every believer!

I realize that what I am about to say has been repeated several times within this chapter. The reason being is because of its importance, which should be in our minds continuously. **The believer must have as their object of faith the Cross an the Finished Work of Jesus Christ!** As believers we must resist any ploy of the enemy (Satan and his minions) from removing us from the **'Cross,'** as the object of our faith!

The last part of the command, which Jesus gave in **Luke 9:23,** is to **'follow Him.'** This is an imperative verb, which commands a continuous and repeated action. Christ can only be followed by the believer, upon his understanding of the **'Cross,'** along with what Jesus Christ accomplished there. It was there (the Cross) where Jesus Christ defeated the enemy and rendered him, and sin, powerless.

> *"Blotting out the handwriting of ordinances that was against us, which was contrary to us, and took it away, nailing it to His cross."*
>
> *"And having spoiled principalities, and powers, He made a show openly, triumphing over them in it (the Cross)." Colossians 2:14-15*

Again, let me reiterate, there is only one way to **'follow'** Jesus Christ on a daily basis, and that is through the leading and direction of the Holy Spirit! And you must also become actively involved in the **'Word!'**

Just as those who were before us, we must, **'embrace'** the promises left us and those that are before us. Today's believer must embrace what Jesus Christ accomplished at the cross and by His resurrection.

> **Your deliverance from sin, sickness and disease was in what Jesus did at the Cross! The 'newness' of life was accomplished there, to give every believer the opportunity to seize, and take hold of, and to 'embrace' what has already been done! Romans 6**

CHAPTER 8

A Pilgrim's Faith is 'An Enduring Faith'

"Therefore endure hardness as a good soldier of Jesus Christ." 1 Timothy 2:3

The phrase, **'endure hardness,'** is derived from the Greek word, **'kakopatheo,'** meaning; to suffer evil afflictions, to be afflicted, to suffer misfortune, to endure, to sustain afflictions.

I am sure that every believer can testify that living by faith draws an attack from the enemy (Satan and his minions). Matter of fact, anyone who tells you that everything is all sunshine and trouble free (after becoming a Christian) is simply not telling the truth. All throughout the scriptures, believers faced one battle after another. That is the bad news. However, the good news is, **Jesus Christ provides the believer with the strength and the 'Word' that brings victory!** With that, Jesus did warn His disciples that they would face some difficult times.

"These things I have spoken unto you, that in me ye might have peace. In the world ye shall have tribulation: but be of good cheer; I have overcome the world." John 16:33

This statement indicates that the believer will be faced with some difficult times from this world! However, it is not the difficult times that will destroy you, but it will be how you handle those times! Without a doubt there is an endurance that every believer will face in their walk of faith. It is through those hard times that allow the believer to enter into the great promises of God! Remember, there is an enemy in world that does not want you (the believer) to succeed in the things that Jesus Christ has provided through the cross! **Endurance** is part of a ***"Pilgrims Faith"***

Allow me to share with you some things that will help get you through those hard times.

You Must Remain Focused!

When the pilgrims set foot on American soil, not everything went well. They faced sickness, disease, and some extremely harsh winters. Yet, they stayed the course. When I think of the path that the patriarchs blazed, it brings this question. What was it that kept the patriarchs of old continuing in the midst of these hard times? Most of them never returned to their old country, even when they had the opportunity (Heb.11:14-15). When they began their search for a better country, they remained separated from their past and remained focused on the land that was ahead!

Sure there were times when a fog tried to cloud their focus, but for the most part, their minds were set on the land that God promised! When a person is moving forward to accomplish a goal, I believe that the main ingredient in fighting the hard times of suffering and misfortune that they faced was (is) keeping their eyes of faith focused on what God had spoken,

John Wooden was unarguably, one of the best basketball Coaches to ever embrace the court! In his coaching career, he guided UCLA to more national championships than any before him and any after him. This is a feat that will probably never be matched, especially in my lifetime. During all of the adversities that his teams faced, while on this great run, he made the following statement, which I believe is one of a great teaching tool for all of. It is certainly a great lesson in hardships.

"Things turn out the best for the people who make the best of the way things turn out!" What a powerful statement! This is certainly a key to overcoming the adversity that arises from time to time, in the walk of faith! This is exactly what the ***'Pilgrims of Faith'*** did; they made the best of where they were, and they continued to look toward where they were going!

When I think about ***'enduring hardness,'*** my mind takes me to the Apostle Paul and his sufferings;

1. **In, stripes above measure**

2. **In, prison frequently**

3. **Facing death often**

4. **Five times received 39 stripes**

5. **Beaten with rods 3 times**

6. **Was stoned once**

7. **Suffered shipwrecks 3 times**

8. **Spent a night and a day in the deep**

9. **In his journeys he faced problems with;**

   A. **Water**

   B. **Robbers**

   C. **His own countrymen**

   D. **With heathens**

   E. **In the city**

   F. **In the wilderness**

   G. **In the sea**

   H. **Among false brethren**

He faced weariness, pain, hunger, thirst, cold and nakedness. This isn't to mention the care he carried for the churches. 2 Cor. 11:24-28. When I read of all that this great man endured, it makes what I (we) have faced in life seem menial.

God revealed to Paul His great **'Grace'** which was sufficient for all that Paul needed!. This resulted in Paul the following statement;

> *"Most gladly therefore will I rather glory in my infirmities, that the power of Christ may rest upon me." 2 Cor. 12:9b*

When I stop and think about all the things that Paul endured, it makes what I am facing seem trivial, in comparison. However, what we may b facing can still be difficult to endure and see our way to victory! The great thing about seeing and examining what others have gone through is that it gives us hope of making it through! When I read the great book of Hebrews, especially chapter eleven, and see all those who lived and died in faith, it brings an encouragement that you and I can make it! Not only was it faith that brought them victory, but it was remaining focused in that faith!

<u>Remain Focused on the Grace of God!</u>

The following are some keys in remaining focused and not giving into your surroundings. In 2 Cor. 12, the Apostle Paul reveals that there was a, **'thorn'** in his flesh. Many have tried to say exactly what Paul's thorn was. I am not here to debate that. However, I believe that Paul made it perfectly clear what the thorn was. He said;

> *"And lest I should b exalted above measure through the abundance of the revelations, there was given to me a thorn In the flesh, the*

*messenger of Satan to buffet me, lest I should be
exalted above measure." 2 Cor, 12:7*

Paul said that it (the thorn) was a **'messenger from Satan to buffet him.'** The phrase, **'to buffet him'** meaning to harass and kick around with the intentions to change Paul's focus! I believe that Paul revealed the methods Satan's messengers used and is found in 2 Cor. 11:24-33. It is important to notice that Paul sought the Lord three times for all of this to depart from him. God's response was;

*"And He said unto me, My grace is sufficient
for thee: for my strength is made perfect in
weakness." 2 Cor. 12:9*

In other words, God was telling this great Apostle, **"Just remain focused my grace."** This grace that God spoke of was, and is, an **'enabling grace.'** This is a grace that is far deeper than **'unmerited favor!'** This **'enabling grace,'** is the way God operates. It is referred to as **'God's operational power!'** It is the **'goodness of God,'** which is now revealed and carried out by the Holy Spirit, who has received that latitude to do what He does because of the, **'cross and the finished work of Jesus Christ!'** To walk in God's **'enabling grace,'** one must have as their faith totally focused on the **'cross and what Jesus Christ accomplished there!'**

Forget About Those Things That Are Behind You!

What, I mean by the above statement is this; what is behind you, should be left there. Stop allowing those things in your past, dictate to your future! Stop visiting there, and avoid the lure to return. This was a problem with Israel, while wandering in the wilderness. They continually thought about Egypt, and how it was better there than the wilderness! That frame of mind got them in trouble on more occasions than one. However, when you the great patriarchs of old, they remained focused on the promises of God that were ahead of them.

Sometimes it can be difficult to let go and forget the past. It can almost be impossible to erase it from your memory. However, to forget them is to be able to keep them behind you. When Abram (Abraham) left the people of Ur, he never returned to the way things were done there! He was in search for a new city; a better country! When, and if, he ever had a chance to return, he didn't. He along with a lot of others endured to the end!

It is important, as a believer that you lose your appetite of the old man (the flesh) and begin to feed the new creature that you are in Christ Jesus! Again, **Don't allow your past to keep you from your future!**

<u>Reach For Those Things Which are Before You!</u>

*"Brethren, I count not myself to have
apprehended: but this one thing I do, forgetting
those things which are behind, and reaching
forth unto those things which are before,"*

*"I press toward the mark for the prize of the
high calling of God in Christ Jesus."*

Everything that Jesus Christ finished (accomplished) at the cross has been made available for the believer today! Just to mention this one thing, which is possibly the greatest of all; ***Phil. 3:13-14***

You may be asking; **'What is before me, because I just can't see it?'** That is really a great question and is asked by many more than you may think. There is in front of every believer an, **'Abundant life also known as the Newness of life!'**

*"The thief cometh not, but for to steal, and to
kill, and to destroy: I am come that they might
have life, and that they might have it more
abundantly." John 10:10*

This **'abundant life,'** Jesus spoke of is a **'newness of life,'** that the Apostle Paul wrote about in Romans chapter 6. The phrase, **'that they might have life, and they might have it more abundantly,'** is speaking of an entirely different way of living. It is living a life under the direction of the Holy Spirit which leads the believer into a life of victory! (Romans chapter 6-8). This abundant life is gauged by what a person possesses, but, it is in the quality of life. It is learning to live putting the sin nature under subject to the Word!

This **'newness of life'** is certainly not trouble-free, nor is it living in sinless perfection. But, it is a life, of overcoming those problems that we all face in everyday living. Actually, the word, **'abundant**, is from the Greek word, **'perissos'** meaning; in the sense of, more exceeding, exceedingly, super-abundantly in quantity and superior in quality. It is a qualitative change that takes place within the believer!

I faith am not suggesting that enduring hard times is an easy thing to do! It takes a lot of discipline and a faith walk to endure hard times and places! I can remember when I entered into the armed forces. During the time of boot camp (basic training), we were presented with various situations that were designed to prepare us for some of the difficulties that were possibly ahead of us. The training was challenging, mentally and physically. However, enduring those times it was those who learned disciplined life that came out on top!

The most important discipline that you will ever face is, **'keeping the cross and the finished work of Jesus Christ before you;** that is, the **'mark and the prize of the high calling of God in Christ Jesus!'**

Only God knows what kind of challenges that are before you! However, I guarantee you, if you will, stay the course and endure those tough times, and keep the **'Cross'** before you, you too will come out on top!

<u>Fight The Urge To Turn Back!</u>

This was one of the things (as I said before) that continually came in the minds of Israel, while in the wilderness. As a nation, almost every time they found themselves in a difficult situation, they murmured, complained, and thought about Egypt! Time and time again, they made reference to the onions and garlic of Egypt. However, there were some, that had the **'pilgrim's'** mindset, particularly, Joshua and Caleb that continued to move forward! While Israel was wandering around in the wilderness, Joshua and Caleb had their minds on the **'land of promise!'**

When facing with hard times you may think about throwing both hands up in the air and quit! If that feeling ever comes your way, and it probably will, resist it and remind yourself of all the **'benefits'** that Jesus Christ has set before you! There also may be times when the comfort of your past may seem inviting! But, remind yourself that the future holds greater blessings than your past ever gave you! So, **'let go of those things that are behind you and get excited about what is before you!**

God desires to take you (the believer) into a deeper walk and a higher place, just as He did for the Patriarchs of old! God did the same thing for Israel bringing them into the **'land of promise!'** There is a **'land of promise for every believer, and I am not talking about heaven (although it certainly is a promise land)! I am referring to His great gift and, that is Jesus Christ! It takes a Pilgrim's Kind of Faith' to get there! Are you ready for the journey of faith that is ahead of you?**

When the hard times come, think on this; *"Many are the afflictions of the righteous: but the Lord delivereth him out of them all." Psalm 34:19*

KEEP YOUR FOCUS (FAITH) ON THE CROSS AND WHAT JESUS CHRIST ACCOMPLSHED THERE!

ABOUT THE AUTHOR

Dr. Baldock is the founder/ president of ***"Gaining the Victory Ministries."*** He began his ministry in March of 1971. In 1973, he began in full time ministry. He is celebrating the beginning of fifty years of ministry. He and his wife, Julie, have been married for thirty-six years. Together, they have seven grown children, Rick, Tammy, Tracy, Rhonda, Alicia, Michael, and Ashley. He and Julie have several grandchildren and great-grandchildren.

Dr. Baldock has pastored nine Churches; four of which he pioneered and built from the ground up. Dr. Baldock also has four earned Doctorate Degrees, and one Doctorate.

He is currently traveling to different church's teaching and preaching the Word of God. He attends the Sanctuary Church in Beech Grove/ Indianapolis, Indiana. Dr. Baldock has spoken at many different venues. He has worked with several well-known ministries. He taught for several years with the International College of Bible Theology and with Midwest Seminary. He has taught undergraduate and graduate school. He also taught at the School of the Prophets in Poplar Bluff, Missouri for about four years and he taught about two to three years at The Lion of Judah in Malden, Missouri. He also traveled to Malawi in East Africa where he helped train over one-hundred and twenty-five church leaders.

Dr. Baldock is a gifted preacher and teacher of the Word. He enjoys training up leaders in the local church and helping restore those who have fallen on hard times and are in need of mentoring. He has authored many books and study helps. He believes that the gifts God has given him should be shared and imparted to others. He believes in everyday, practical teaching which will reveal the application of the Word of God in the everyday living. He is a strong believer in the fact that everything you will ever need is supplied through **'The Cross and the finished work of Jesus Christ.'** He believes that the **'Cross'** is the means and **'Jesus Christ'** is the source of all that you have need of.

Dr. Baldock is available to speak and or teach at your local church or, conference, along with leadership training. If you would like for Dr. Baldock to come and speak at your church or conference, awnd if you would like more information about his books, cd's, dvd's, and teaching tools you can get in touch with him at;

Gaining The Victory Ministries

Dr. R. Michael Baldock

P.O. Box 648
Spencer, Indiana 47460;
You can email us at
gainingvictoryministries@gmail.com

You can also visit our web page at
gainingvictoryministries.org

RESEARCH MATERIALS

The Hebrew Greek Key Study Bible King James Version
1984, 1991 By AMG International, Inc. Revised Edition 1991
The Expositor's Study Bible King James Version Concordance

Jimmy Swaggart Ministries
P.O. Box 262550
Baton Rouge, LA. 70826-2550

The New Strong's
Expanded Exhaustive Concordance Of The Bible
James Strong, LL.D.., S.T..D.
Expanded With The Best of Vine's Dictionary
Of Old & New Testament Words
The Preacher's Outline & Sermon Bible
On Hebrews 11:1-40 NIV
Leadership Ministries Worldwide

P.O. Box 21310
Chattanooga, TN. 37424-0310